TARGET
LITERACY

Roger Lane

OXFORD
UNIVERSITY PRESS

Great Clarendon Street, Oxford OX2 6DP

Oxford University Press is a department of the University of Oxford.
It furthers the University's objective of excellence in research, scholarship,
and education by publishing worldwide in

Oxford New York

Athens Auckland Bangkok Bogotá Buenos Aires Calcutta
Cape Town Chennai Dar es Salaam Delhi Florence Hong Kong Istanbul
Karachi Kuala Lumpur Madrid Melbourne Mexico City Mumbai
Nairobi Paris São Paulo Shanghai Singapore Taipei Tokyo Toronto Warsaw
with associated companies in Berlin Ibadan

First published 2000

Reprinted 2000

ISBN 0 19 831462 0

Designed and typeset by Mike Brain Graphic Design Limited, Oxford

Printed in Spain by Graficas Estella SA.

Contents

To the Reader

Most school students would like to improve their reading and their writing, but many are not sure how to go about it. Some do not think it is possible because they do not think they are good enough! Well, this book tries to deal with only the things that matter and it tries to explain them in a straightforward way. It gives you practice in the kind of questions and tasks that you have to tackle at the end of Key Stage 3.

The activities in the book have already been tried successfully by students in English lessons, so they should work for you and your friends as well. The reading texts have been chosen to make you laugh, make you sad, make you angry and make you think!

Good luck at getting your English in shape!

Acknowledgements

Thanks to the students of Bedwas Comprehensive School, Tonyrefail Comprehensive School and Ysgol Gyfun Penweddig for trialling the units and providing samples of reading and writing.

Roger Lane

Bella

Bella

Bella was special. I thought so anyway, though I never let on. She was Harold's sister, one year younger than him and the same age as me. She had brown skin and very light blonde hair, but deep brown eyes. Her parents christened her Dorabella. They were always doing things like that. But we called her Bella.

We were in the same class at school, but girls had to sit on the other side of the room from boys, so I couldn't talk to her then. And we had separate playgrounds. We didn't meet on Sundays either, because their family went to a posher chapel than ours. Sometimes in the evening, in summer, though, when we were still in our Sunday best, the whole family would go for a walk along the Meadow. Then we'd all meet. Bella's mam and dad were on speaking terms with ours, though our dad was on the Works and Bella's dad was in business as a builder, and fancied himself a bit.

We used to pass by, hot and tight in our clothes (Bella used to have her hair pinned back till it pulled her eyebrows up) and wishing we could have an ice cream or a drink of pop. Our dads would raise their hats and our mams would say, 'Good night, then.' Harold and I would shake our fists at one another and Bella would screw her nose up at me.

'What are you doing?' asked her mother.

'Got a fly on my nose,' answered Bella.

'Walk straight, girl,' said her dad.

I'd sneak a look round and put my thumb to my nose at Harold, until I felt Dad's finger in my back.

'Stop acting the goat, lad.'

That was Sunday. It couldn't end too soon. But Saturday, that was different. On Saturday we all got together and no one watched what we were doing. Well, not much anyway.

Sometimes on hot summer days we'd go down to the Old River. The Old River was how it used to be, with rapids and a sluice, where the water tumbled down about twenty feet, foaming and boiling. The banks were all hung over with grass and weeds. The New River wasn't new any more. It was donkey's years since they cut the new channel and put locks in so that the flat boats could get up to the Works. It was deep, dirty and dangerous and if you went on the lock gates, the keeper might chase you off.

The Old River was deep, too, in places, but there were sandbanks where you could wade out.

There's More!

It was dirty, too, and in summer when the sun got on the water, it stank. Our parents told us off for going there, but we thought it was just the job.

The way down to the Old River was through the back lanes off the main road, past a little wood, keeping well clear of the houses at Tunnel Top, because their gang were too tough for us, and then full tilt down Gorse Hill. Gorse Hill was steep and green with short slippery turf and dotted all over were the gorse bushes with bright yellow blossoms. When the sun went down, the hill looked as though it were on fire. Right at the bottom was an old tow-path, broken here and there where the water had got in under the cinder track, and almost disappearing in bushes and weeds. We'd charge down Gorse Hill at full speed.

The trick was to keep your legs going faster than your head so you didn't come a cropper – and then pull up short so you didn't run straight into the river.

We sat on the bank of the Old River one day, watching the boats pass through the locks across on the new cut. It was so hot the sweat was running down my nose, even lying still.

'Tell you what,' said Jammy, jumping up. 'Let's go in the river.'

'Don't be dopey,' said Harold. 'We haven't got our cossies.'

'I'm going in anyway,' said Jammy, peeling his shirt off.

'You're kidding.'

'Want to bet?' said Jammy, and ducked behind a bush. Next minute we heard a splash and he was in the water.

'Come on,' he yelled. 'It's smashing.' We looked round.

'Are you windy, or something?' shouted Jammy, kicking up his heels and spraying water all over the place. We didn't wait any longer. Harold and I picked a bush each and stripped down. Just then I heard a gasp from Harold. Bella was taking her frock off.

'Hey, Bella. You can't do that!'

'Get off. I want to come in as well,' she answered.

'You can't!'

'Why not?'

'Course you can't. Girls don't.'

'Ah, don't be mean, Harold. Let her come in if she wants to,' I said. 'Eh, Jammy?'

There's More!

9

I looked round to Jammy for support, but he pretended he hadn't heard me.

'You stay on the bank and watch our clothes. We don't want kids from the locks pinching 'em,' said Harold.

So Bella stayed on the bank and looked glum while we went in the water. It was cool and smooth as milk, though the sun was hot. I jumped from a sandbank and went right down. The water was green and I could see the sunlight showing through in a great yellow patch. I burst up again in the air and got a mouthful as Harold slapped the water with his arms. I slapped back. Jammy joined in. We made such a racket we didn't hear Bella shouting at first.

'Hey, come out. It's Constable Collins.'

'You're kidding.'

'Not. He's coming up from the locks.'

We panicked. Have you ever tried to run, when you're up to your waist in water? But we had no time to stop. If PC Collins told our parents, we were in real trouble. We charged off up the bank. Have you ever tried jumping gorse bushes when you're dressed in nothing but good intentions? In ten seconds flat we were half way up the hill and hiding behind some bushes.

Bella climbed up behind us more slowly.

'Where is he?' whispered Harold.

'You keep down. Your bum's showing,' said Bella. With my head pressed down in the grass I couldn't see her face, but I could tell from her voice she was enjoying this. We lay there trying to keep out of sight and clear of the gorse bushes at the same time. I could see Jammy wriggling about.

'What're you doing?'

'Trying to get my shorts on.'

'How did you get them?'

'Picked 'em up on the run.'

'Trust you, Jammy –' A few yards away, Harold raised his voice.

'You, Bella. Where are you?'

The bushes parted. Bella flopped down by my side. Without a word, she passed me my shorts and singlet.

'Did you get our clothes?' asked Harold from the other side of the bush. She smirked, and winked at me.

'Sorry, Harold. I was in such a rush I couldn't pick them all up.'

'What am I going to do?' yelled Harold.

'Hey, shut up. PC Collins'll hear you.'

'What am I going to do?'

'You'll have to wait till he's gone, won't you? Unless you want to borrow my nicks.'

'Don't be disgusting,' snarled Harold. He glared at her and crouched down behind a gorse bush. It was painful for him in more ways than one.

Next Saturday we gave the Old River a miss. But we went down there again before the summer was out. We had a swim now and then. And Bella came in with us. And Harold kept his mouth shut.

I'm keeping my mouth shut, too. PC Collins was nowhere near the Old River that day. Harold doesn't know that, and I'm not telling him.

ROBERT LEESON

The Reading Question

How does the writer, Robert Leeson, make this simple childhood adventure into a good, lively story?

Talk about

❋ the character of Bella
❋ the way the boys behave towards her
❋ the boy telling the story and how he gets on with Bella
❋ your favourite moments of the story
❋ what you think of the story, especially the ending.

See if you can find examples from the story to back up your opinions.

The Grammar Class

Paragraphs and Sentences

If you want to improve your writing, you must try to build good, clear **sentences** and **paragraphs**.

Look back at *Bella* to check how sentences are punctuated with commas and full stops. Look also at the way *Bella* is organized into sections called paragraphs.

Paragraphs

Paragraphs give shape to a piece of writing and help the reader's eyes move around the page easily. Here are some tips on writing good paragraphs.

❋ Each paragraph starts with an extra space on the left of the first line of writing. This is called an indentation.
❋ Each sentence starts with a capital letter.
❋ Commas show readers where to pause during a sentence.
❋ There is a full stop at the end of each sentence.

Check that you know what paragraphs look like by counting them in *Bella*. How many paragraphs are there before the mother speaks? You should count three paragraphs. Now look at the first paragraph and count the number of sentences. You should find seven full stops and therefore seven sentences. (Paragraphs vary in *Bella* from between one and eight sentences long.)

Task 1

Here is a paragraph from *Bella*. Show what you know about paragraphs, full stops and capital letters. Write out the paragraph properly. Try to do it without looking back at the story. Don't forget to start with an indentation. Commas have been put in for you. You need to add eight full stops. Check that capital letters are in place at the start of each sentence.

So Bella stayed on the bank and looked glum while we went in the water it was cool and smooth as milk, though the sun was hot I jumped from a sandbank and went right down the water was green and I could see the sunlight showing through in a great yellow patch I burst up again in the air and got a mouthful as Harold slapped the water with his arms I slapped back Jammy joined in we made such a racket we didn't hear Bella shouting at first

When should you start a new paragraph?

There is no strict rule, but you might find this advice useful .

A paragraph should start with a key sentence, called a **topic sentence**. The topic sentence introduces the main business of the paragraph. Think about starting a new paragraph for a new person, new place, new time, new idea, new speaker.

Task 2

Here are some incomplete topic sentences from *Bella*. Your task is to complete each one of them. Test your memory. See how close you can get to the topic sentences in the story.

1 We were in the same class at school, but...
2 Sometimes on hot summer days...
3 The Old River was deep, too, in places, but...
4 We sat on the bank ...
5 Next Saturday...

Task 3

Write a paragraph of five sentences about something unusual that happens to a friend. It can be a true tale or you can make it up. Start with something like 'My friend John was...'.

Stop after five sentences. Remember the indentation at the start of your paragraph and the capital letter and full stop in each sentence.

Simple Sentences

Simple sentences are important. If you understand what simple sentences are, you can go on to build other types of sentences with skill.

So what is a sentence?

A sentence is a group of words that makes complete sense by itself. Here are some tips on writing good sentences.

❋ The words must be in a sensible order.
❋ The punctuation must be correct.
❋ The sentence should contain a verb (an action or 'doing', 'being', 'having' words).

Task 4

To help you with sentences and verbs, here are some simple sentences from *Bella*. They need a capital letter, a full stop and a verb. Write the sentences out properly. Find them in the story or work them out for yourself.

1 bella ✎✎✎ special
2 she ✎✎✎ brown skin and very light blonde hair, but deep brown eyes
3 her parents ✎✎✎ her Dorabella
4 we ✎✎✎
5 we ✎✎✎ off up the bank
6 bella ✎✎✎ up behind us more slowly

You have probably been told not to start sentences with 'and' or 'but'. Good advice, even though Robert Leeson breaks this rule! (He perhaps does so because it's the way his story-telling character speaks.)

Task 5

Find three sentences from *Bella* that start with 'and'. Also find three sentences that start with 'but'. Copy the six sentences, missing out 'and' or 'but'. Don't forget to use correct punctuation.

The Writing Challenge

Autobiographical Writing

Think of the times you have spent with your friends over the years. Think of one or more incidents that stand out and how you might tell this as a story. It might be about things that have happened recently or things that happened years ago. Make sure you introduce your friends fully into the tale.

The challenge

* write about yourself and at least one of your friends
* write in paragraphs with indentations
* use a capital letter at the start of each sentence
* use a full stop at the end of each sentence
* do not start any sentence with 'and' or 'but'
* write at least one simple sentence in each paragraph.

Writing Support

Here are two pieces of writing by the same pupil. They are about different occasions. You should be able to see that the second one is better for a number of reasons.

Example A

It was a cold wet and windy day, and I just didn't want to get up from my bed. I had had a lie in as it was, I had to be up bright and early to get to Bridgend at 7.30 a.m. I had got all my gear together the night before, but I wanted to check through it once more before I left to make sure I had not forgot anything, as it was I had forgot a spare swimming cap and a spare pair of goggles. It was soon time to go, my mum wished me good luck then we went.

Example B

There they all were climbing up that big tower of a climbing frame, hanging upside down from the middle, reaching the top and shouting 'you can't get me.' There I was, sitting on the swing, wishing it was me at the top of the climbing frame, thinking it should be me winning the races across the fields. It was all my fault. I just couldn't do it, I couldn't bring myself to join, because I knew they would all make fun of me.

In Example A, Ceri has started her story without thinking a great deal about the words and sentences that she uses. In Example B, however, she is really involved in the story and she gets us involved too. There is more descriptive detail and more feeling in Extract B and Ceri is obviously thinking more about her writing.

In your own writing, think of what will get the reader interested.

Writing Frame

Your teacher will give you a writing frame like this one to help you plan your work.

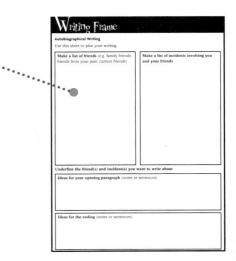

Unit 2
Gone is Gone

Text

Gone is Gone

In the north country, where grass grows on the roofs of the cottages, there once lived a farmer who was not pleased with his lot in life. 'I do more work in a day than you do in three,' he said to his wife almost every noon-time and evening when he came in from the fields. 'I toil and sweat, ploughing and sowing and harvesting, while you laze around the house.'

At last his wife grew tired of hearing this talk. 'Very well, husband,' she said. 'Tomorrow I will do your work, and you can do mine. I'll go out to cut the hay, and you can stay here and keep the house.' 'Good,' the husband said, and he

Task 1

Copy out the following sentences based on the story and place 'and' or 'but' in each gap.

1 He churned and he churned, ✎✎✎ the butter would not come.
2 He went out the cottage door ✎✎✎ down into the cellar to get some ale.
3 He ran up the cellar steps as fast as he could, ✎✎✎ he was too late.
4 The cow didn't want to go onto the roof, ✎✎✎ he pulled and coaxed her.
5 He climbed down off the roof ✎✎✎ hurried back into the cottage.
6 The wife ran up and cut the rope with her scythe, ✎✎✎ the cow fell to the ground.

Complex Sentences

Do you write sentences with conjunctions like 'if' and 'while'?

If you do, you will certainly be a better writer. Sentences joined by conjunctions like these are called **complex** sentences. They can help you to describe and explain things more accurately in your writing. This kind of conjunction can appear at the start of a sentence or in the middle. Here are some more examples:

when	where	although	since	because
for	as	before	after	so

I toil and sweat, while you laze around the house.

If I do your work, you must do mine.

Task 2

Copy out the following sentences and fill in each gap with a conjunction to complete a complex sentence.

1 The husband thought that he would begin by churning the cream, ⬟⬟⬟ there would be butter for the porridge at dinner.
2 The pig came into the cottage, ⬟⬟⬟ the farmer had left the door open.
3 ⬟⬟⬟ he was grinding some oatmeal, he heard the cow mooing in the barn.
4 He thought it would be much easier ⬟⬟⬟ he could only get the cow herself onto the roof.
5 The cottage was full of chickens, ⬟⬟⬟ he had left the door open again.
6 ⬟⬟⬟ the wife came up the hill, the first thing she saw was the cow hanging from the roof.

Putting Conjunctions into Practice

Task 3

To show that you know how to use conjunctions, make up a sentence of your own for at least six different conjunctions. You should end up with six (or more) separate, interesting sentences.

Choose from and, but, if, while, when, where, although, since, because, for, as, before, after, so.

Do you sometimes leave out conjunctions? It is a bad habit to leave out conjunctions and to try and join sentences with commas. It is called **comma-splicing**. Don't write like the example at the top of the next page.

I went to the match last night, it was a lousy game, the referee didn't help, he kept booking our players, Hughes got the ball in the net, the ref disallowed it.

Task 4

Re-write the paragraph below and improve it by using conjunctions like 'and', 'but', 'so', 'as' etc. Don't forget to control your sentences with full stops. You should end up with four or five sentences if you stick to what is written below, but you could try to extend the story from one paragraph to two by using your imagination!

My friend just went straight in, he started throwing punches, he got stopped by our teacher, we were moved to another bus, that bus was full of screaming girls, I hated it, I had a mighty big headache, I felt a tap on my back, it was Mr Roberts, he just looked at me.

Do you ever use 'and' and 'so' too often and forget to end sentences?

The skill lies in knowing when to end a sentence. Keep your sentences reasonably short. Don't write like the example below.

My friend Sarah came round last night and we went up to my room and listened to some CDs and then my brother came in and started annoying us so I yelled at him and then my mum came upstairs and said …

Task 5

Look at the paragraph below, this time there are too many conjunctions! Re-write the paragraph, cut out some of the conjunctions and put in some full stops and capital letters instead of some of the commas. You should again end up with four or five controlled sentences. Then, continue the story with an extra paragraph of your own.

I woke up on Christmas Day and it was still dark, so I tried to go back to sleep, but I couldn't, so I looked at my pillowcase and it was full of presents and I pulled one out and I wondered what it was and then Mum and Dad woke up...

The Writing Challenge

Imaginative Writing

Imagine that, like the farmer in *Gone is Gone*, you have had a terrible day. Write a story about your day. It doesn't have to be true and it doesn't have to be you!

The challenge

❋ write a lively story
❋ write in paragraphs with indentations
❋ use a capital letter at the start of each sentence
❋ use a full stop at the end of each sentence
❋ use commas for pauses during longer sentences
❋ control the use of 'and', 'but' and 'so'
❋ use 'if' and 'while' and other conjunctions.

Writing Support

Getting Started

If you are stuck, use the writing below as the opening to your story.

As soon as I walked down the stairs, I just knew it was going to be one of those days. I sat at the table and baby Nicky threw a spoonful of marmalade on my clean pair of trousers. I didn't have enough time to change, so I went to school with stained trousers.

I was soaked by the time I reached the bus stop, because it was raining cats and dogs…

The Ending

Try not to spoil your story with a stupid moment, especially at the end. Think of an ending which rounds off the terrible day with a punchline. Here's one that does it well.

Oh well, the day didn't turn out as bad as I expected, because it turned out worse! I can cope with Annie for a day, but I just this second discovered that she's coming back tomorrow. Aaaargh!!!!

Writing Frame

Your teacher will give you a writing frame like this one to help you plan your work.

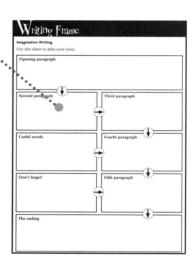

Text

At Techniquest, you can:

freeze your own shadow

fire a rocket

launch a hot air balloon

see yourself on television

CYBER LIBRARY

DISCOVERY ROOM

LABORATORY

SCIENCE THEATRE

PLANETARIUM

play a harp without strings

120 INTERACTIVE EXHIBITS

film your own animation

PUZZLES

tame a tornado

CHALLENGES

lose yourself in a maze of mirrors

and much, much more...

29

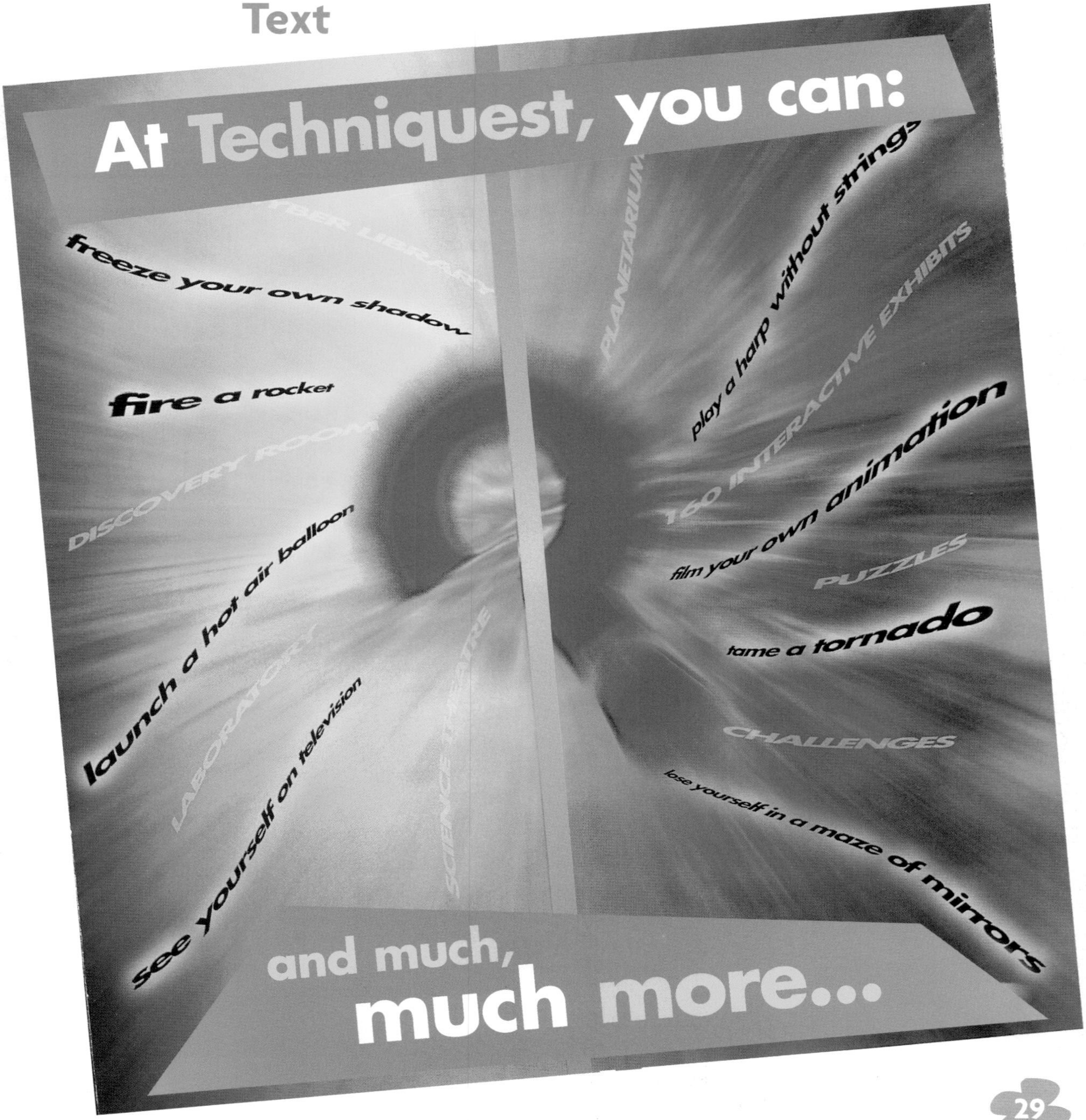

Other facilities

SCIENCE THEATRE
- a state of the art 100-seat Science Theatre for an ever-changing programme of science shows. Phone or check our website for latest events.

PLANETARIUM
- a 30-seat hollow sphere where you can see the stars by day and tour the solar system. Star shows are not suitable for under 5 s.

DISCOVERY ROOM
- a circular room offering a bird's eye view of the exhibition area. It contains our collection of curiosity boxes on topics as varied as fossils and bridge building.

The Planetarium, Theatre and Discovery Room are usually available during school holiday periods and weekends only, subject to availability, and incur an additional charge.

SCIENCE SHOP
For the latest gifts and gadgets, pocket money toys and books, visit our science shop! Also open for shoppers not wishing to visit the exhibition.

CAFÉ
An excellent range of refreshments, snacks and drinks always available.

Facilities for the disabled are provided throughout the Techniquest building.

Discover the excitement of science at Techniquest,

a new style of hands-on environment that is neither museum nor funfair but has the best of both for inquisitive minds of all ages.

Techniquest is a great family outing, providing 2-3 hours of family fun with friendly staff to help you! Thousands of schools have also attended our term-time educational programmes which meet National Curriculum requirements.

NEW!

CYBER LIBRARY

Surf the net and explore CD-Rom packages in our brand new Cyber Library.

Allow at least a couple of hours for your visit. And while you're here, enjoy the other attractions of the Cardiff Bay Millennium Waterfront, including the Visitor Centre, Harry Ramsden's, Sports Cafe, Norwegian Church Arts Centre, Lightship 2000 and the new Mermaid Quay shopping complex.

At Techniquest no-one says "Don't touch!"

OPENING TIMES

Monday - Friday	9.30am - 4.30pm
Saturday, Sunday & Bank Holidays	10.30am - 5.00pm

Last admission 45 minutes before closing. Techniquest is closed for a few days at Christmas. Techniquest reserves the right to alter admission charges without prior notice.

ADMISSION CHARGES 1999

Adults	£5.00
Children (5-16 years)	£3.75
Children (under 5)	Free
Concessions	£3.75
Family Ticket (2 adults & up to 3 children)	£14.50
Friends of Techniquest annual family season ticket	£40.00

An additional charge applies for Planetarium (75p) and Discovery Room (50p) sessions.

Group visits

Discounted rates apply for pre-booked groups of 10 or more people by telephoning 01222 475 476.

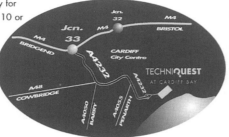

HOW TO FIND US

BY CAR

From outside Cardiff - Leave M4 at junction 33 (Cardiff West Services) and follow the A4232 to Cardiff Bay.
From City Centre - Follow signs to Cardiff Bay.

BY BUS

No 7/7a every 15 minutes from Churchill Way
No 8 from Heath Hospital or Central Bus Station, stand W3

BY TRAIN

Direct train from Cardiff Queen Street to Cardiff Bay station

PARKING

There is supervised parking at the rear of the Techniquest building.

To contact us: Techniquest   Stuart Street   Cardiff   CF1 6BW
T 01222 475 475   F 01222 482 517   email: gen@tquest.org.uk

Visit the Techniquest web site on www.tquest.org.uk for the latest information.

CARDIFF BAY
Europe's most exciting waterfront development

MILLENNIUM PRODUCTS

Designed at Techniquest © 1.99

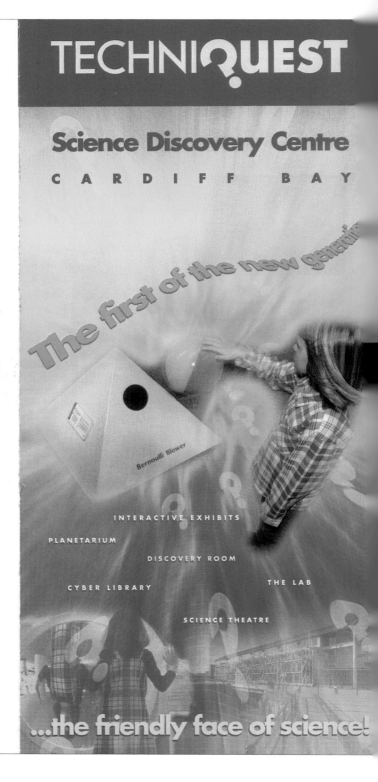

TECHNIQUEST

Science Discovery Centre

C A R D I F F   B A Y

The first of the new generation

Bernoulli Blower

INTERACTIVE EXHIBITS

PLANETARIUM

DISCOVERY ROOM

CYBER LIBRARY

THE LAB

SCIENCE THEATRE

...the friendly face of science!

The Reading Question

The leaflet says 'Discover the excitement of science at Techniquest'. How successful is the leaflet in making science seem exciting and in tempting young people to visit Techniquest?

Talk about

* the information about things to see and do at Techniquest
* the use of photographs, colour, headings, and layout
* how the words and sentences try to persuade you to visit Techniquest.

See if you can find examples from the leaflet to back up your opinions.

The Grammar Class

Types of Sentence

Statements, commands, exclamations, and questions are all different types of sentences. How much do you know about each type?

Statements

A **statement** is a sentence that gives information to a reader. A statement ends with a full stop. Most sentences are statements. Some are short, and some are longer. Some statements are presented in note form with a dash.

Techniquest is a Science Discovery Centre in Cardiff Bay.

Discovery Room – a circular room offering a bird's eye view of the exhibition area.

33

Task 1

Find the following statements on the leaflet and copy them out fully, with a full stop at the end of each one.

1 Science Theatre – a state of the art...
2 Facilities for the disabled...
3 Techniquest is closed...
4 Thousands of schools...
5 Star shows...

Exclamations

An **exclamation** is usually a short sentence that shows strong feelings. An exclamation is followed by an exclamation mark, which looks like this '!'.

Task 2

There are five exclamation marks on the leaflet. Find them and copy down each full exclamation.

1 Techniquest is a great family outing, ...!
2 N__ !
3 For the latest gifts and gadgets, ...!
4 At Techniquest no-one says ...!
5 Techniquest ...the friendly ...!

Commands

A **command** is a sentence that expects someone to do something. If the command is sharp, the sentence should end with an exclamation mark to show strong feeling. Some commands, though, are polite instructions, while other commands try to persuade us to do something. The Techniquest leaflet has a lot of polite commands!

Discover the excitement of Science at Techniquest...

Allow at least a couple of hours for your visit.

Look at the part of the leaflet on page 29 and see how the designer has turned one long statement into a series of short commands.

At Techniquest, you can:

freeze your own shadow

tame a tornado

fire a rocket

Task 3

Find these five commands from the leaflet and copy them down. Make sure you put a full stop at the end of each one.

1 Surf ...
2 Allow at least ...
3 Phone or check ...
4 Lose yourself ...
5 From City Centre – Follow ...

Questions

A **question** is a kind of sentence that asks for information and needs an answer. A question ends with a question mark. The answer will usually be a statement.

Where can we park our car? (question)

There is supervised parking at the rear of the Techniquest building. (answer)

Task 4

Now write down five questions of your own to ask about Techniquest. Don't forget the question marks. You do not have to answer the questions.

Task 5

Make a snappy advertisement for Techniquest. Draw a box like the one below and copy out the text in it. You have only four sentences to fit between 'Techniquest' and 'Science Discovery Centre, Cardiff Bay'. You must think of one statement, one exclamation, one command, and one lively question (e.g. 'How much do you think you know about Science?'). You can use them in any order! Try to use your own original sentences and ideas.

Techniquest

Science Discovery Centre
Cardiff Bay

The Writing Challenge

Letter Writing

Pretend you are the head of science at your school and you are organizing a school trip for Year 7, 8 or 9 to Techniquest. Write a letter to parents of your chosen year group telling them about Techniquest and explaining how it will help their children with their school work.

Work out the important practical details for the trip — date, time, cost, transport, etc.

(If you live a long way from Cardiff ... pretend you don't!)

The challenge

* write a clearly organized letter with correct layout
* make the letter long enough to inform and persuade parents
* express yourself politely to parents about pupil behaviour
* write brightly, but do not copy sections of the leaflet word for word
* use a range of sentence types.

Writing Support

Here are some questions that pupils and parents might ask about the school trip to Techniquest. You may find it useful to read them and think about them before you write your letter.

Pupils' questions

A trip to a science museum? Won't it be boring?

Will we have to sit down and listen?

What will we be doing?

Will we be doing any work?

Will we be allowed to go around Techniquest on our own?

Parents' questions

How much will it cost?

How do I know my child will be safe?

What is the educational value of the trip?

What are the arrangements for pupils getting back home?

Writing Frame

Your teacher will give you a writing frame like this one to help you plan your work.

Writing Frame

Letter Writing
Use this sheet to plan your letter.

School address
Date

Dear Parent,

Paragraph 1 (include the practical details about the trip)

Paragraph 2 (include some information about Techniquest)

Paragraph 3 (stress the educational value of the trip)

Paragraph 4 (lay down ground rules about pupil behaviour)

Paragraph 5 (final persuasion – why this trip will help children with their school work)

Yours sincerely,

Unit 4
Poetry

Text

A PROUD OLD MAN (GRANDPA)

They say they are healthier
   than me,
Though they can't walk to the
   end of a mile.
At their age I walked forty at night
   to wage battle at dawn.
They think they are healthier
   than me.
If their socks get wet they
   catch cold,
When my sockless feet got wet,
   I never sneezed,
But they still think that they are
   healthier than me.
On a soft mattress over a spring
   bed
They still have to take a sleeping
   pill.
But I, with reeds cutting into my
   ribs
My head resting on a piece of
   wood,
I sleep like a baby and snore.

PAUL CHIDYAUSIKU (ZIMBABWE)

WARNING

When I am an old woman I shall wear purple
With a red hat which doesn't go, and doesn't suit me.
And I shall spend my pension on brandy and summer gloves
And satin sandals, and say we've no money for butter.
I shall sit down on the pavement when I'm tired
And gobble up samples in shops and press alarm bells
And run my stick along the public railings
And make up for the sobriety of my youth.
I shall go out in my slippers in the rain
And pick the flowers in other people's gardens
And learn to spit.

You can wear terrible shirts and grow more fat
And eat three pounds of sausages at a go
Or only bread and pickle for a week
And hoard pens and pencils and beermats and things in boxes.

But now we must have clothes that keep us dry
And pay our rent and not swear in the street
And set a good example for the children.
We must have friends to dinner and read the papers.

But maybe I ought to practise a little now?
So people who know me are not too shocked and surprised
When suddenly I am old, and start to wear purple.

JENNY JOSEPH

SHONI ONIONS

He comes with autumn, when the leaves flake
from the rusty branches. His old bicycle
itself's a twisted tree, its creaking black
hung heavy with the long strings ripened full.
He is at the end of things; a sure sign,
the sad smile wrinkled in his golden skin.

There used once to be more of him, they spoke
a tongue that was the one half of a code
between old neighbours, a key to fit the lock
of cousins' speech, distanced but understood.
He sells in English now; his customer
or he mislaid the other words somewhere.

The boats that took our coal to Brittany
once brought him back; surely they don't still run?
Only old custom's sake now brings him by,
each year the same, a little older grown,
a taste sharp as nostalgia on his wares
startling the tongue; stinging the eyes to tears.

SHEENAGH PUGH

THE RIVER IN SUMMER

Me and Grangad on the beat-up bikes,
Down to the river as lazy summer dust
Rises and thickens the air,
Scrunching the gravel under the wheels,
With dappled sunshine playfully peeking through the treetops.
Cut-down fishing nets poking spitefully into tender backs,
Through tattered, bumpy old rucksacks,
Brambles scratching at brown knees.
Out of the shadows, off the bikes,
And over the scorched grass to the bank.
Off with the T-shirts and shorts,
Squelch through hot, sticky mud,
Before slipping into the cool flurry of glassy river,
With lemon-juice freshness,
Gravel, ice-like and sharp on tender feet,
Feet branded with sandal-strap whites.
Bask in the cool shaded water.
Wallow and splish-splosh,
Or keep very still and feel the silver minnows,
Slipping with timeless magic over slimy limbs.
But –

Example B

A 90 year old lady lived in a small cottage in the country. She had lived in the same cottage for 60 years. She got married to her husband from this cottage and had had her children there. She has lived alone since the death of her husband and her children each have married and moved away, but she would not leave her home. She had been asked to go and live with her daughter and her family but she would not...

Example C

My grandad likes to know what is happening in the world so he likes to watch the news. He has got a large apple tree out in the front of his garden and every summer I go to pick. He has always told me stories about my uncles and aunties. He told me a story about my Uncle Johnny who had a fight with a boxer outside the Piccadilly pub in Caerphilly. They both couldn't beat each other up so my uncle took him home for tea and cakes...

Have you got any ideas for your own writing now that you have read these short pieces? You need someone to write about, preferably someone you know. Then you can write about what they do, what they say and how they look. You can repeat their tales of the past. The examples above show how it can be done, but you perhaps can do even better if you use descriptive detail to create a picture of your character in words.

Writing Frame

Your teacher will give you a ·········•
  writing frame like this one
to help you plan your work.

Writing Frame

Descriptive Writing
Use this sheet to plan your story.

Description of your elderly person (notes or sentences)

Typical things they might say

Key moments or events in the story

Opening paragraph (notes or sentences)

Ideas for the ending

Unit 5
The Gold of Lies

Text

THE GOLD OF LIES

Characters: Stranger; Maid-servant; Inn-keeper; Thief.

In front of an inn. There is a bench or something similar somewhere on stage.

*Enter **Stranger**, carrying a lump of gold.*

Stranger *(To audience)* I am a traveller. After a long journey across the mountains I've arrived here in a country no one has ever visited before. Who knows what strange people and customs I may come across? I must be careful. But fortune has been kind to me. I found this lump of gold in the mountains, and when you've got gold you can always get anything else you want. But since I've never been here before I can't trust anyone. Who knows what villains and liars I might meet?

*Enter **Maid-servant**, carrying bottles of beer which she puts down on the bench.*

Maid-servant Hello. What's that you've got there?

Stranger *(To audience)* She's seen my gold! – *(He hides the gold. To Maid-servant)* Nothing. Nothing at all.

Maid-servant Nothing? That's strange. I could have sworn I saw you holding something.

Stranger   Well, yes, I was. It's gold. But I don't want anyone to know about it.

Maid-servant Gold?

Stranger   Yes. *(He shows it to her.)* See? I found it in the mountains. But don't tell anyone I've got it.

Maid-servant But suppose they ask me?

Stranger   Say you haven't seen anything.

Maid-servant But I did see it.

Stranger   Yes, I know. But pretend you didn't. Tell a lie.

Maid-servant Tell a lie? What's that?

Stranger   Eh?

There's More!

51

Maid-servant I've never heard of telling a lie before.

Stranger You've never heard of telling a lie?

Maid-servant No.

Stranger *(To audience)* Hmn. The girl's obviously a half-wit. – *(To Maid-servant)* It's perfectly simple. When you say something that isn't true it's called telling a lie.

Maid-servant I thought it was called making a mistake.

Stranger No, it's making a mistake if you do it without meaning to. If you do it deliberately it's called telling a lie.

Maid-servant Deliberately making a mistake? But what's the point of that?

Stranger *(To audience)* I've never met anyone so stupid. I really think she doesn't know what telling a lie is. Either that or she's a very clever liar indeed. – *(To Maid-servant)* Never mind. It doesn't matter. Are you the maid-servant at this inn here?

Maid-servant That's right.

Stranger Where's the inn-keeper? I want a room for the night.

*Enter **Inn-keeper**.*

Inn-keeper Who's this?

Maid-servant It's a stranger. He's been explaining to me about telling a lie.

Inn-keeper Telling a lie? What's that?

Stranger *(To audience)* Him as well? – *(To Inn-keeper)* Are you the inn-keeper here?

Inn-keeper That's right.

Stranger I'd like a room for the night.

Inn-keeper Certainly.

Stranger I hope your locks are strong. I'm very worried about thieves.

Inn-keeper Oh, there's no need to bother about that. If I see a thief I'll come and warn you.

Stranger Well, that's very kind, but how will you know if he's a thief or not?

Inn-keeper I'll ask him.

Stranger But if he's a thief he's hardly likely to tell you, is he?

Inn-keeper They always do.

*Enter **Thief**.*

Here comes somebody now. – Excuse me, are you a thief?

Thief Yes, I am actually.

Inn-keeper *(To Stranger)* There you are, you see. – *(To Thief)* What are you doing around here?

Thief I've come to try to steal some of your beer.

Inn-keeper Oh, yes? And how do you think you're going to do that?

Thief I was going to wait until you weren't looking.

Inn-keeper That's clever. Yes, I hadn't thought of that.

Stranger *(To audience)* They're mad, all of them!

Inn-keeper We'll have to make sure we keep an eye on it. – *(To Stranger)* Now then, what was it you wanted? A room for the night?

Stranger That's right. How much will it cost?

Inn-keeper Well, let me see now...What have you got?

Stranger I'll pay you in gold.

Inn-keeper Gold?

Stranger That's right.

Inn-keeper What's gold? I've never heard of gold before.

Stranger What's the matter with you people? Haven't you heard of anything?

STEVE FITZPATRICK

The Reading Question

The opening of *The Gold of Lies* is puzzling. How successful do you think the writer is in making it mysterious and entertaining?

Talk about

* the Stranger (what he has been doing and what kind of person you think he is)
* the funny conversations that take place about lies, gold and stealing
* why it would be entertaining to see it acted out as a play
* what you think might happen in the rest of the play.

Look for the lines in the playscript that you think are mysterious or entertaining and use them to back up your opinions.

The Grammar Class

Verb Tenses

Verbs always give information about time – whether it is in the **past**, the **present** or the **future**. To do this, verbs have to alter their forms. This is what we call the **verb tense**.

Past Tense

I found this lump of gold in the mountains.

Present Tense

I am a traveller.

Future Tense

How much will it cost?

Task 1

Copy each of the following sentences from *The Gold of Lies* and write 'past', 'present' or 'future' by each one.

1 Fortune has been kind to me.
2 I'll (I will) ask him.
3 Here comes somebody now.
4 They're (They are) mad, all of them!
5 He has been explaining to me about telling a lie.
6 I'll (I will) pay you in gold.
7 I want a room for the night.
8 But I did see it.

Choosing the Right Tense

There are lots of different past tenses to choose from. Look at the four different examples in the sentences below.

The Stranger had walked for days. He was approaching a village at last. He thought to himself 'I have arrived!'

The boundaries between the present and future tenses are not always clear cut.

In fact, in the example below, the past runs into the present and the present runs into the future.

Now I have reached my room I am going to hide my gold!

Task 2

Copy out the Stranger's opening speech below and fill each gap with the correct verb form. Try to do this task without looking back at the playscript. The examples above will help you.

> I ✎✎✎ a traveller. After a long journey across the mountains I've ✎✎✎ here in a country no one ✎✎✎ ever visited before. Who knows what strange people and customs I ✎✎✎ come across? I ✎✎✎ be careful. But fortune ✎✎✎ been kind to me. I ✎✎✎ this lump of gold in the mountains, and when you've ✎✎✎ gold you ✎✎✎ always get anything else you want. But since I've never ✎✎✎ here before I can't ✎✎✎ anyone. Who knows what villains and liars I ✎✎✎ meet?

Short Verb Forms – the Apostrophe

In *The Gold of Lies* there are many examples where the use of an **apostrophe** makes a short form of a verb. These are called **contractions**. You probably know most of them already, but here is a chance to check some out.

'I have' can be shortened to 'I've'

'he is' becomes 'he's'

'do not' becomes 'don't'

In nearly all cases the apostrophe replaces the missing letters. 'Won't' (will not) breaks the rule! Short verb forms (or contractions) represent the way people often speak.

Task 3

Find at least ten examples of short verb forms from *The Gold of Lies* and write them down. Write down the longer forms as well. Here is one to get you started.

what's   what is

Negatives

Negative words have an important role to play in some sentence. Here are some examples:

not or n't   no   never   no one

But, beware, there are right and wrong ways of using them.

Don't use **double negatives**. When you do, you will be saying the opposite of what you mean! Look at the example below.

I've not got no money.
(This could be taken to mean 'I've got some money'.)

She didn't give me none.
(This could be taken to mean 'She gave me some'.)

Negatives are important, but they should be used properly like the two examples below.

I've not got any money. She never gave me any.

I've got no money. Mum gave me none.

Fortunately, the characters in *The Gold of Lies* use negatives properly, so there are lots of 'correct' examples to spot. Look at this example from the Stranger's first speech.

After a long journey across the mountains I've arrived here in a country no one has ever visited before... But since I've never been here before I can't trust anyone.

Task 4

The Stranger, the Maid-servant, the Inn-keeper, and the Thief may be odd, but they do not use double negatives! Each of the sentences below is a wrong version of sentences spoken by the characters. Write out the correct sentences.

1 But I don't want no one to know about it.
2 But don't tell no one I've got it.
3 Say you haven't seen nothing.
4 I've never met no one so stupid.
5 I was going to wait until you weren't not looking.
6 I hadn't never thought of that.
7 I've never not heard of gold before.
8 Haven't you heard of nothing?

The Writing Challenge

Writing a Playscript

Write your own playscript, using two, three or four characters and one scene only. In other words, when the dialogue starts it must be developed at some length before the scene ends. You must choose an everyday situation that you can work with like a visit to the hairdresser or taking your pet to the vet where conversation takes place and some interesting things could happen.

The challenge

- ❧ write your own playscript of good length (at least two or three sides of paper)
- ❧ use the correct playscript layout (look back at *The Gold of Lies*)
- ❧ create two, three or four clearly different characters
- ❧ keep the playscript in one place and time
- ❧ use stage directions to set the scene and to tell the actors what to do and how to say things
- ❧ include at least one longer speech by a character
- ❧ give full attention to punctuation.

Writing Support

If you are stuck for ideas, then use one of these openings to get you started.

The Staff Meeting

*In the staffroom. The **Head** is waiting to start a staff meeting.*

Head   Right then, are we ready to begin?

Mr Inklemann   (*In the backroom, distant voice*) One minute, I'm just getting a cup of coffee.

Head   (*Slightly disgusted*) Huh, we'll begin. Right then, top of the agenda the boys' toilets and the recent spate of vandalism. How do we propose to deal with this?

Mrs Jones   Perhaps...

Mr Inklemann   Sorry, have I missed anything?

Head   Sit down, Mr Inklemann!

***Mr Inklemann** sits down.*

Head   (*Continuing*) Carry on, Mrs Jones.

Mrs Jones   Perhaps if we er …

***Mr Inklemann** stands up.*

Head   (*Getting fed up*) What is it now, Mr Inklemann?

Mr Inklemann   Sorry, Headmaster, I wonder if we could turn the heating off … I can't hear Mrs Jones because of the blowing noise …

Lifting Spirits

Matt*, *Anna* and *Rose* *are passengers in a lift.

Anna   Which floor?

Matt   Anna, you know which floor. I go there every day.

Anna   I know, I was just trying to be polite.

Matt   Oh, sorry.

Rose   (*Nervous cough*)

Suddenly there is a creaking sound and the lift stops dead.

Anna   What the hell was that?

Matt   It was the lift stopping.

Anna   I know it was the lift stopping!

Matt   I mean … between floors.

Anna   I know it's between floors!

Matt   Well … probably between the fourth and fifth floors.

Anna   It doesn't matter which floors!!

Rose   (*Another nervous cough*)

Writing Frame

Your teacher will give you a writing frame like this one to help you plan your work.

Unit 6
Tough Luck

Text

This story is an extract from the novel Tough Luck by
Berlie Doherty. Mr Bead, a school teacher, is concerned
about one of his pupils. He visits the father in the hope of
finding out what is worrying the boy.

TOUGH LUCK

Joe Bead set off for Twagger's house that night after school. . . He had to knock on the door several times before it was opened. The smell of tobacco smoke and beer rushed out to meet him. Mr Sanders, unshaven and still in his vest and braces, peered out at him.

'Thought you was the telly-man, way you was knocking,' he said. 'What d'you want?'

'I'm Mr Bead, from Hill Bank School. I'm Michael's form teacher. Can I come in, Mr Sanders?'

'What's he got up to now?' grinned Mr Sanders. 'Been knocking teachers about?'

'Can I come in, Mr Sanders?' Mr Bead repeated. He didn't feel much like going in to the stench of that house, but he didn't

There's More!

want to carry on this conversation out in the street either, with a circle of toddlers round his knees.

Mr Sanders went back into the house, and Mr Bead followed him. There was no sign of Twagger. The living room carpet was stained with swirls of alcohol and cigarette burns. In the centre of the room was a wooden coffee-table with two opened beer cans, and a litter of magazines from the job centre. Mr Sanders settled himself on the brown settee, picked up one of the cans, and stretched his feet across the table. In the corner of the room an American film blared on the television. Cars chased each other, screeching, across the screen.

'Mr Sanders,' said Mr Bead at last. 'I'm very concerned about your son.'

'Oh, aye?' The man's eyes flicked across to him then back to the screen. He sucked at the beer can.

'He's not been coming to school, for one thing.' Mr Bead had to shout above the loud film track.

'Doesn't like it, probably.'

'I'm afraid that doesn't give him the right to miss school,' Mr Bead said. He tried to smile. 'Don't like it myself, some of the time.'

Twagger's dad snorted scornfully. 'I'm sorry for you. Don't know you're born, you lot.'

'Michael doesn't seem to be very happy at the moment,' Mr Bead tried again. 'I was wondering if we could talk about that.'

Mr Sanders drained his can noisily. 'How d'you mean, talk about it? Talk about what?'

'About Michael, basically. What can you tell me about him that might explain his behaviour at the moment?'

There was a long pause. The front door opened and closed

again. Light steps ran up the stairs. 'Is that him now?' asked Mr Bead.

'What's he been telling you?' shouted Mr Sanders. 'What you come sneaking and prowling round here for anyway? I'm not choosing to tell you anything about my son, because he *is* my son, and because he's no concern of yours.'

'Well, he is my concern.' Mr Bead was alarmed at the aggression in the other man's voice. 'While he's at school and in my form he is my concern.'

'And while he's not at school he's mine, and as you've just been telling me that he never comes to school anyway I suggest you get out of here. Now.'

He stood up, and Mr Bead jumped out of his chair.

'I'd like to see Michael before I go,' he said.

'And I'd like you to shove off now, because you're getting up my nose. Clear off, will you?'

'I'd like your assurance that Michael will be coming to school in future, Mr Sanders.' Mr Bead backed down the hall, glancing anxiously up the stairs.

'Don't you worry, he'll be coming to school, if I have to get out of bed in the morning and take him there myself. Now clear off.'

He opened the door and Mr Bead plunged out into the wonderful sleety air of the street.

BERLIE DOHERTY

The Reading Question

How does Berlie Doherty, the writer, build the tension and excitement in this story?

Talk about

❀ what Mr Bead, the teacher, sees when he meets Mr Sanders, Twagger's father, and enters the house
❀ the conversation between Mr Bead and Mr Sanders
❀ Twagger, who we do not see in this part of the story
❀ the way the story is written and the way this particular incident ends.

See if you can find examples from the story to back up your opinions.

The Grammar Class

Direct Speech

Do you know how to use speech marks accurately?

'Well, sort of...'

'I know what they look like, but...'

Speech marks enclose the actual words spoken by a person in a story. The words spoken by someone are called **direct speech**.

'Thought you was the telly-man, way you was knocking,' he said.

The direct speech always ends with a punctuation mark (just before the speech marks close).

'I'd like to see Michael before I go,' he said.

Normally this is a comma, though a question mark or exclamation mark is often needed instead. You only use a full stop if the direct speech is followed by another sentence. When you do Task 1, look at the different examples to see how this rule works.

Task 1

Copy out the following sentences and put in the speech marks. The other punctuation has already been supplied.

1 What's he got up to now? grinned Mr Sanders.
2 Can I come in, Mr Sanders? Mr Bead repeated.
3 He's not been coming to school, for one thing. Mr Bead had to shout above the loud film track.
4 I'm afraid that doesn't give him the right to miss school, Mr Bead said.
5 What's he been telling you? shouted Mr Sanders.

The layout of the examples in Task 1 is quite straightforward. But you may want to use other techniques like:

* breaking a speech into two parts
* using words other than 'said'
* missing out the speaker's name when it is clear who is speaking.

Tasks 2, 3 and 4 will give you some practice at doing this.

Task 2

Copy out these sentences and carefully place speech marks where they are needed.

1 Mr Sanders, said Mr Bead at last. I'm very concerned about your son.
2 Michael doesn't seem to be very happy at the moment, Mr Bead tried again. I was wondering if we could talk about that.
3 Light steps ran up the stairs. Is that him now? asked Mr Bead.

Task 3

Find five words in the story that are used instead of 'said'. Then think of another five words of your own that could also be used.

In several parts of the story, Berlie Doherty deliberately misses out a reference to the speaker. In this example it is obvious that it is Mr Bead who is speaking (asking a question). But how do you think he is saying it?

'I'm Mr Bead, from Hill Bank School. I'm Michael's form teacher. Can I come in, Mr Sanders?'

He is probably quite polite at this point, although he doesn't say please! Let's try adding 'enquired the teacher cautiously'.

'I'm Mr Bead, from Hill Bank School. I'm Michael's form teacher. Can I come in, Mr Sanders?' enquired the teacher cautiously.

Now try a few of your own. Don't forget that there are always different ways of saying the same words!

Task 4

Who is the speaker of each of these sentences? How is each one said?

Choose at least three and write them out fully like the example on the previous page.

Remember, for questions 1, 3 and 5 you will need to change the full stop at the end of the speech into a comma.

1 'Doesn't like it probably.'
2 'About Michael, basically. What can you tell me about him that might explain his behaviour at the moment?'
3 'And while he's not at school he's mine, and as you've just been telling me that he never comes to school anyway I suggest you get out of here. Now.'
4 'And I'd like you to shove off now, because you're getting up my nose. Clear off, will you?'
5 'Don't you worry, he'll be coming to school, if I have to get out of bed in the morning and take him there myself. Now clear off.'

Report Writing

Imagine you are the representative pupil on the school council for your year group. You have been asked by the head teacher to write a report entitled 'Improving School' which will be presented to the school governors. Your ideas should take into account the needs of all pupils. It is most important that you are polite and positive in the way you write, or else the governors simply will not take you seriously.

The challenge

* write a formal report with headings
* write about several school issues, including subject lessons
* show good sense of what it is possible to change and what it is not
* write politely about teaching and non-teaching staff
* impress the governors by using clear, controlled sentences and accurate punctuation
* make sure you double check your spelling.

Writing Support

Here are some comments from pupils about school. You could use these in your report, or interview people you know to get their opinions.

'I like practical lessons, when we use computers and make things, but there aren't enough lessons like that. There's too much listening to teachers.'

'School is a really friendly place. It's where I meet my friends. It's so good that it should be open until at least 7 o'clock. It seems daft for the place to be closed by 4 o'clock.'

'I love learning languages, but I'm slowed down because lots of people in the French class can't be bothered to do their work, so the lessons have to go slowly. I'm not a swot, but I do get bored.'

'What's in school for me? I'm no good at maths and English, so everybody reckons I'm thick. Teachers shout at me. I don't feel part of the place.'

'I really fancy doing photography, but there's no chance until the sixth form.'

'The older kids have got a common room, but we have to stand outside at lunchtime. They say we'd wreck a common room if we had one.'

Writing Frame

Your teacher will give you a writing frame like this one to help you plan your work.

Unit 7
Aliens Kidnapped Me

Text

CLOSE ENCOUNTER: Welshman tells of medical tests by creatures in octagonal helmets

ALIENS KIDNAPPED ME IN A SPACE SHIP

By Michael Settle

DAVID THOMAS is living in fear after he was kidnapped by aliens who told him: 'We'll be back'.

Star trekkers from across the universe flew him into deep space where they examined him and asked him for his eyes.

Then they brought him back to Earth and left with the chilling message: 'We will see you again.'

Now Mr Thomas is recalling his experiences in a new book about Close Encounters of the Fourth Kind, Alien Abductions from Planet Earth.

Mr Thomas, now 28, who lives in Pwllheli, Gwynedd, was on his way home in the early hours of the morning when he heard what seemed like the humming of an electricity generator from a road-side field.

There's More!

He stopped his car and walked down a muddy track to investigate. It was then he was snatched by the aliens and whisked away.

UFO investigator Philip Mantle said last night that Mr Thomas' case was one of the most convincing he had ever heard.

'There is no doubt he believes that he experienced what happened,' said Mr Mantle.

Mr Thomas suffered frightening nightmares and his family were so worried for his health that his mother drove him to Oxford to meet UFO investigators.

Mr Mantle said: 'A year later when I went to interview him, he still had burn marks on his wrists from the experience. He was still very perturbed about what had happened.'

And the worst thing was that the aliens told him that they would come back for him. He told investigators: 'They have chosen me, they have instructed me and they are coming back for me.'

Mr Thomas said his close encounter began when he was grabbed by the shoulder by an alien and led through a gap in the hedge by the edge of the field.

They had nothing like the friendly features of ET. They were like a throwback to the alien horror movies of the 1950s.

They wore octagonal helmets, grey suits, gold belts and straps and black knee boots and gloves.

The alien craft was 20ft high and was hovering about two feet off the ground. It was domed and disc-shaped and had antennae or stabilizers poking out and a window and drawbridge at the front.

On board he saw Jupiter and Saturn flashing by before the

vessel docked with a mother ship.

He was taken for a medical and they asked him if they could take his eyes for further examination, but he refused.

Mr Thomas, which is not his real name, told investigators: 'They told me they came from a planet beyond the constellation of Lyra, that they breathed pure oxygen and disliked the polluted atmosphere of earth.'

And they questioned him about the USA and NASA because they had captured a Voyager probe.

When he was dumped back on earth he was found reeling in the road by a passing policeman, who took him home.

Today, nine years later, Mr Thomas is married and still lives in Pwllheli. Mr Mantle says he does not want to talk about what happened to him anymore.

'But it has totally changed his life. He has developed talents for poetry and music and he is an avid campaigner on green issues.'

The Reading Question

The newspaper report 'Aliens kidnapped me in a spaceship' was actually published in the *Wales on Sunday* newspaper.

How much, if at all, do you believe the story of the aliens?

Talk about

* what David Thomas says about what happened to him
* what UFO investigator Philip Mantle knows of the story
* the way the report has been written and organized
* the picture (the artist's impression of the aliens)
* your own explanations and your own opinions on the story.

Look closely at the newspaper report and try to use examples from it to back up your opinions.

The Grammar Class

Agreement

The word **agreement**, in grammar, means that all the different parts of a sentence fit together correctly, according to the rules of standard English.

Standard English is the kind of English you find in text books, newspapers and you hear on the TV news.

Which of these sentences uses correct English?

* I seen an alien.
* I has seen an alien.
* I have seen an alien.

In the first sentence 'seen' has been confused with the simple past tense 'saw'. 'I saw an alien' would be OK.

In the second sentence, 'I' does not agree with 'has'.

However, in the third sentence, 'I have seen an alien' everything agrees! To be technical, the verb 'have' agrees with the subject 'I'.

Task 1

From each set of brackets choose the verb that agrees with the subject of the sentence.

1 David Thomas (do live/is living) in fear after he (be/was) kidnapped by aliens.
2 They (has/have) chosen me, they (have/has) instructed me and they (is/are) coming back for me.
3 They (was/were) like a throwback to the alien horror movies of the 1950s.
4 When he (were/was) dumped back on earth, he (was/were) found reeling in the road by a passing policeman, who (takes/took) him home.
5 Today, nine years later, Mr Thomas (is/be) married and still (lives/live) in Pwllheli.
6 It (has/have) totally changed his life.

Task 2

Copy out and complete the grid below.

Start with the subject column on the far left.

Then choose a verb from the top of each column that agrees with the subject.

Write it in the box. Keep going until all the boxes have been filled.

The first one has been done for you.

	present	past	present	past	present	past
	am/are/is	was/were	do/does	did	have/has	had
I	am			did		had
you				did		had
he she it				did		had
we				did		had
you				did		had
they				did		had

Task 3

The aliens sent the message below to the earthlings. Write it out properly in standard English by making the verb agree with the subject of each sentence.

We has come in Peace. We does not wish to fight. We be very friendly and kind aliens. We likes your planet very much. You is very lucky to have *Eastenders* on four times a week.

Using Adjectives to Compare Things

Adjectives are descriptive words. A **comparative adjective** describes by comparing two things.

The first alien was strong, but the second alien was stronger.

Another way of forming a comparison is by using the word 'more'.

If the adjective is already a long word, such as 'intelligent' or 'beautiful', adding '-er' is not an option because it would be too clumsy to say 'intelligenter' or 'beautifuller'.

One alien was more intelligent than the other, but which one was more beautiful?

However, there is also a third alien! When you have more than two things to compare you need a different form of adjective, called a **superlative adjective**. You form a superlative adjective by adding '-est', or by using 'most'.

The third alien was the strongest, most intelligent and most beautiful of them all!

Look out for the following spelling rules.

* Muddy becomes 'muddier' and 'muddiest'.
* Big becomes 'bigger' and 'biggest'.
* When you make a comparison you cannot use '-er' and 'more' together. So you should not write 'more friendlier'!
* When you want to use a superlative you cannot use '-est' and 'most' together. So you should not write 'most ugliest'!

Task 4

Copy out the sentences and fill in the gaps with comparative and superlative adjectives.

1 This was the ⬚⬚⬚ experience of David Thomas' life.
2 ET was ⬚⬚⬚ than the aliens that Mr Thomas saw.
3 UFO investigator Philip Mantle said that Mr Thomas' case was one of the ⬚⬚⬚ he had ever heard.
4 Do you think that the aliens think that Earth is ⬚⬚⬚ or ⬚⬚⬚ than their own planet?
5 Mr Thomas is now nine years ⬚⬚⬚ than he was when he met the aliens.

Best, Worst and Others

There is a small group of comparative and superlative adjectives that behave oddly.

Here are some examples:

Comparatives	Superlatives
worse	worst
better	best
less	least
more	most

Task 5

Copy out and fill in the grid below with the correct pattern of comparative and superlative adjectives. Choose from the eight examples on page 80.

	Comparative	Superlative
good		
bad		
some		
little		

Task 6

Copy out the sentences below and correct the comparative and superlative adjectives.

1 The spacecraft was more bigger than a double decker bus.
2 The most youngest of the aliens was called Baby Alien.
3 Mr Alien was pleasanter than Mrs Alien.
4 The aliens thought that Earth was more dirtier than their own planet.
5 David Thomas was the frighteningest thing the aliens had ever seen!

The Writing Challenge

Writing a Mystery Story

Write a mystery story, without blood or a haunted house! Think of a situation — you might observe a spaceship landing or you might face a time-warp. Build up the atmosphere, revealing information slowly, but holding back the true mystery. Try to avoid the obvious by creating a surprise — perhaps the aliens are friendly, perhaps the ghost is scared, perhaps there is no monster! Include some dialogue (direct speech with speech marks) in your story — perhaps those aliens don't speak English!

The challenge

- ❇ write a story with an atmosphere of mystery
- ❇ include dialogue in the story, with accurate use of speech marks and layout
- ❇ use descriptive language to create your characters and the place in which the story is set
- ❇ organize your paragraphs and control your punctuation.

Writing Support

Which one of these openings is the best for grabbing your attention?

You could use one of them as the start of your own story.

The Ghost at the Crossroads
by Chris Culshaw

NOBODY FROM the village would go near the crossroads after midnight. Everyone said the place was haunted. Lots of people said they had seen a white figure there – a horrible one-eyed woman with a big black cat.

Men in Black
– *A Real Story by Jenny Randles*

In January 1976, 17 year old Kerry Wellbrook was on her way home from work when she saw strange red and amber lights 'dancing' over a reservoir about half a mile away. Moments later she found herself looking up at a circular craft 20 or 30 feet across, rotating like a spinning top no higher than the rooftops above her head.

GHOST RIDERS

BY ALEX GUTTERIDGE

Not on Highwayman's Hill. Of all places to break down, please don't let it be here...

Nule

BY JAN MARK

The house was not old enough to be interesting, just old enough to start falling apart. The few interesting things had been dealt with ages ago, when they first moved in...

Writing Frame

Your teacher will give you a writing frame like this one to help you plan your work.

Writing Frame

Writing a Mystery Story
Use this page to plan your story.

Outline of the situation	Characters

Details of the place where the story is set

Important steps, twists and moments in the story

Key things said by the characters

Opening line

Last sentence

Unit 8
Kick it Out

Text

Looking back

Racism was once all over football like a rash. Many supporters from the 1980s will be able to recall shocking scenes of bananas being thrown onto the pitch and crowds chanting racist slogans.

Henrik Larsson, Sweden

Henrik, did you experience racism while you were growing up in Sweden?

'Yes, in school I experienced some racism, because back then it was unusual to have a black kid at school, I was one of the few.'

How did you feel?

'At first I didn't understand what they meant because there were words I had never heard before. Then I started to understand what they were saying and I started to stand up for myself.'

Is racism a big problem in Sweden?

'I think that it is becoming better, because when I was young there was a lot of it, not only against black people but against foreigners who had come to Sweden to work, because they had trouble in their own countries. I think that it's about to change, I hope so.'

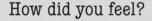

84

Where's racism from?

At Show Racism the Red Card we believe that there are lots of different reasons for racism existing in our society. We also believe that racism can grow through ignorance and stupidity.

Gianfranco Zola,
Italy

'I think that the main reason for racism is ignorance. All children must know that there is no difference between people of any race.

It is a great thing to have a conversation with people of different backgrounds. You can compare your ideas with theirs, you can be a better person. In the world there are many people who have different opinions and if you can collect more ideas yourself, it is good because you can have more experience.

I think it is the same thing in football. I read many newspapers, some of them say, that it is not good that footballers from outside this country are playing in 'our' leagues. I think that this is incorrect. We had the same thing in Italy, when many foreign players came to play in our leagues. If you want to learn, the foreign players can teach you many new things and if you are interested in football and you want to grow you can use your ideas

with those of others so you can be a better player.

I personally learnt a lot from players who came to play in Italy. When Maradona came, when Platini came to Italy, I got some ideas from them. This is a good thing for youngsters. I think in the next few years we will have many, many good young players in England.'

show racism

the **red card**

Fighting back

Whether it's in the stands or in the classroom, we believe that everybody has a duty to challenge racism if we are to stop it spreading. But how? Below some footballers give their ideas.

Frank Sinclair,
Jamaica

What would be your message to black people facing abuse?

'The worst thing that you can do is keep it to yourself. The best thing to do is to share the problem. When we got race hate mail at Chelsea, we didn't hide it, we showed it to all the other players and everybody would say don't worry about people like that.'

Ryan Giggs,
Wales

Did you come across racism at school?

'Yes, the odd bit, both in primary and secondary school. It's similar to bullying and as a young kid it affects your whole life. It's not nice when it's happening to you.'

What advice would you give to young people getting abuse?

'Talk to someone, a teacher or a parent can help. Don't leave it too late and don't let the people who are bullying you rule your life.'

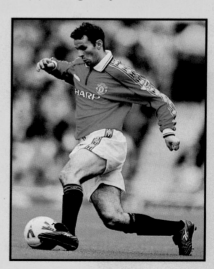

Nathan Blake,
Wales

'In our area we used to get into fights all the time when I was a kid, that's the way that I was brought up. I was told that if someone calls you a name you deal with it in the best way you know how; so I'd fight.'

What advice would you give to young people who hear people telling racist jokes?

'You usually find with kids that they go with the flow and start laughing because their friends are laughing. They should try to be a bit stronger and show them that it's not funny. There's no need for it. I think that really and truly deep down everyone knows that it's wrong.'

Getting Grief?

If you or one of your friends is facing racist abuse or bullying then the first thing is to decide to do something about it.

Nobody needs to suffer in silence. Think about telling somebody that you can trust, maybe a friend or teacher. Is there a school council or union where you are? Get them involved; get as many people as you can on your side.

Remember the racists are in the wrong and they can be isolated.

The Reading Question

How does the reading material from 'Kick it Out' help the fight against racism?

Talk about

❈ some of the comments from the footballers
❈ the statements and advice from the writers of the magazine
❈ the way the material is organized into sections, with headings
❈ the choice of material and the different kinds of people who might read it.

See if you can pick out key information from the magazine material to back up your opinions.

The Grammar Class

Pronouns

A **pronoun** is a word that you use for someone or something, instead of using a name. Pronouns are very useful, important and common, but you have to be careful and clear in the way you use them. Most of them are easy to recognize.

Personal Pronouns

Here are some personal pronouns:

I   me   you   he   him   she   her   it
we   us   they   them

In the example below, the pronoun 'it' refers back to 'racism' in the first sentence.

Show racism the red card. Kick it out.

Task 1

Copy out these sentences and fill in the missing personal pronouns.

1 Gianfranco Zola says, '~~~ think that the main reason for racism is ignorance.'

2 Nathan Blake says, 'You usually find with kids that ~~~ go with the flow and start laughing because their friends are laughing.'

3 Ryan Giggs says, 'It's not nice when it's happening to ~~~.'

4 Henrik Larsson says, '~~~ think that ~~~ is becoming better, because when ~~~ was young there was a lot of ~~~, not only against black people but against foreigners who had come to Sweden to work because ~~~ had trouble in their own countries.'

5 Remember the racists are in the wrong and ~~~ can be isolated.

Task 2

Complete each pair of sentences below. Show that you know how to use pronouns correctly. Don't be afraid to give your own opinions.

1 My favourite sportsman is ...
   He ...

2 My favourite sportswoman is ...
   She ...

3 My favourite sport is ...
   It ...

4 Sport can be ...
   You ...

Indefinite Pronouns

Here are some other kinds of pronouns:

anybody (or anyone)   somebody (someone)

everybody (everyone)   nobody (no one)

anything   something   everything   nothing

These pronouns are called **indefinite pronouns** because they are just a body or a thing without a name.

The manager said, 'Everybody is as sick as a parrot.'

Reflexive Pronouns

Here are some **reflexive pronouns**:

myself   yourself   himself   herself
itself   ourselves   yourselves   themselves

They are called reflexive pronouns because they reflect like a mirror.

He looked at himself.

Task 3

Use an indefinite or reflexive pronoun to complete each of the sentences below. The sentences use ideas from the magazine articles.

1 ≈.≈.≈ has a duty to challenge racism.
2 ≈.≈.≈ needs to suffer in silence.
3 Think about telling ≈.≈.≈ you can trust.
4 The worst thing you can do is keep it to ≈.≈.≈.
5 Decide to do ≈.≈.≈ about it.
6 'I started to stand up for ≈.≈.≈.'

Task 4

There are mistakes in each of these sentences. Re-write each one correctly.

1 Yourself and Sian have been picked for the county squad.
2 Ourselves are the champions!
3 Please pick myself for the team next week.
4 The strikers helped theirselves to easy goals. (check spelling)
5 We have only ourselfs to blame for the defeat. (check spelling)
6 Ian injured hisself when he scored. (check spelling)

Capital Letters

You know that a **capital letter** should be used at the start of a sentence, but they should also be used for the first letter of names.

This includes names of people, places and football clubs.

George Edwards, England and Aston Villa

Task 5

List ten names beginning with capital letters from the leaflet. Then list five more common types of name needing capital letters. Here is one to get you started.

Months (February)

The Writing Challenge

Writing a Magazine or Newspaper Article

Write an article for a magazine or newspaper on a topic you are very interested in or feel very strongly about. Whatever you decide to write about, make sure that you try to pass on some detailed knowledge of the topic to the reader. You could try to get the reader to take an interest in your 'hobby'. If you write on a topic you feel strongly about, make sure you explain fully the situation that you wish to argue against.

You can write your article as a single, straightforward piece of writing in paragraphs or you can design one or two pages of a magazine imaginatively for your topic.

The challenge

- ❋ write a bright, interesting article that informs and persuades the reader
- ❋ use standard English with not many errors
- ❋ organize your article neatly on the page.

Writing Support

If you are stuck for an idea, here are just a few topics you could write about.

Computers

Are computers just a way of wasting time and getting fat or do they educate you? Do you learn new skills?

Music

More and more young people are learning to play the guitar or electronic keyboards. Your instrument may be something more classical? How do you go about learning to play a musical instrument?

Looking After a Pet

Is your pet a cuddly kitten or is it something not so common? How do you look after your pet? What skills and knowledge do you need to be an effective pet owner?

Sport

This is still the main way of passing the time for most young people. Is your sport big or have you found a minority sport? Are you an expert at karate or a star at snooker? Do you get out of the house and travel long distances to watch or play sport? Do you watch sport on TV? Should there be more women's sport on TV?

Pollution

Pollution doesn't just mean global warming and holes in the ozone layer. What about local pollution when the river has a slick of chemicals floating down it? What about the smell coming from the local chemical factory making people ill?

Writing Frame

Your teacher will give you a writing frame like this one to help you plan your work.

Writing Frame

Writing a Magazine or Newspaper Article
Use this page to plan your article

Headline

Author of article

Picture (?)

Third and fourth paragraphs to include quotations from experts or the general public

Sub-heading

Opening paragraph

Second paragraph

Final comment

Unit 9
Oakwood
– The Ultimate Theme Park Experience

Text

There are no boundaries on fun at Oakwood.

Whatever your age, you can be sure there is something for you. Splash Out on the wild and wet Waterfall ride or set sail for calmer waters on the boating lake.

A WORLD OF FAMILY FUN

Something for everyone! Join the jolly crew aboard The Pirate Ship, test your toboggan skills on The Alpine Bobsleigh or beat the chequered flag on the junior and senior Go-Kart courses.

MAXIMUM CHOICE FOR EVERYONE!

Vertigo is the closest sensation to free flight imaginable: a 50 metre fall at speeds reaching 110kph in just 1.5 seconds - **THE FLIGHT OF YOUR LIFE!**

You'll never come down

Megafobia is the ultimate coaster challenge: Over 900 metres of terror track with a heart-stopping 25 metre first drop, eleven crossovers and an exhilarating break from over 45kph to stop. **Dare you ride it?**

Snake River Falls

Snake River Falls combines the thrill of white-water rapids with exhilarating outdoor and tunnel chutes - a wet 'n wild ride not to be missed!

MEGAFOBIA
THRILLS BEYOND FEAR

Oakwood

THE CUTTING

NEW FOR 99

the BOUNCE

U
UGH
JGH?

RIDE DATA:

MEGAFOBIA
HEIGHT (1st Drop) - 25m' Speed: 88kph, 2.75 G-force
☆ BEST WOODEN ROLLERCOASTER IN THE WORLD

VERTIGO
HEIGHT - 50m' Speed: 110kph, 3 G-force
☆ BEST NEW SKYCOASTER 1997

Snake River Falls
HEIGHT - 15m'
☆ EUROPE'S LARGEST WATERCOASTER

THE BOUNCE
HEIGHT - 47m' Speed: 70kph, 4 G-force
☆ UK'S FIRST SHOT & DROP TOWER COASTER

The Bounce

There will be no countdown! Feel your adrenaline rise as you wait for the big blast; watch the treetops rocket into view just to disappear beneath your feet; float in suspension 47 metres above ground! Then plummet to earth - before the ultimate 'bounce' back up into the air! The Bounce is the UK's only Shot and Drop tower coaster reaching speeds of up to 70 kilometres per hour and 4 G-force in less than two seconds!

DGE OF FEAR

97

UNLOCK THE DOORS TO IMAGINATION

When it comes to a fun-packed family day out, the sky is the limit at Oakwood! In Playtown, children are free to be whatever they want! Join the convoy at the Truck Depot, earn your wings at our Junior Flying School or captain your own mini-Pirate Ship! Tots will feel like giants in this special kid's world! Fly, sail or soar to the best day out imaginable!

Sheriff Jake has a warm welcome for critters at his Music Hall Puppet Show in Jakestown. Kids can pan for gold, board the Emerald Express on the Goldmine Ride and even play in Jake's Backyard.

KIDS RULE!

KIDS RULE AT OAKWOOD! KIDS RULE AT OAKWOOD! KIDS RULE AT OAKWOOD! KIDS RULE AT OAKWOOD! KIDS RULE AT OAKWOOD!

One big day out aboard Playtown's Little Big Wheel, traditional Carousel and Tractor Ride!

Clown around on the Kiddiecoaster – the training ground for future coaster nuts!

Enjoy creature comforts at our "hand's on" Playtown Farm where cuddles galore are in store!

CRUCIAL FUN FOR LITTLE ONES

EASY TO FIND! NO LIMITS

Oakwood is clearly signposted off the A40 between Carmarthen and Haverfordwest.

Open daily at 10am from 27 March 1999 until 26 September 1999. Only 2 hours from Bristol

- Pre-booked and confirmed coach parties and groups (minimum number 20): £8.95

  All group entries to be paid with one transaction.

- Education/School parties: Teachers/Adults/Children during term time £7.95

  One complimentary ticket issued for every 10 children to be used at the discretion of the organiser.

- Prices include rides and attractions listed in this brochure with the exception of Vertigo as a supplementary charge applies. £10 per flight (three flyers), £15 per flight each (two flyers), £30 per flight (one flyer). Booking is advisable

Family ticket for 4 people	£39.95
Adults & Children 10 years and over	£10.95
Children 3-9 years	£9.95
Children 2 and under	FREE
Senior Citizens over 60 and disabled	£8.95

Vertigo Bookings & General Park Enquiries: (01834) 891373
(During Park opening hours)

Bookings Hotline & Brochure Requests: (01834) 891484
(9am-5pm, Mon-Fri)

We reserve the right to withdraw the use of any activity, ride or show for any technical, operational or other reason beyond our control. Certain size, height & health restrictions apply.

Visit our Website for the latest news and offers.
http:\\www.oakwood-leisure.com

Prices valid March-September 1999.

24HR INFORMATION LINE: (01834) 891376

Oakwood, Canaston Bridge, Narberth, Pembrokeshire, SA78 8DE.

The Reading Question

How does this leaflet try to attract visitors to Oakwood?

Talk about

* some of the things you can do when you visit
* the way the leaflet is written to persuade you
* who the leaflet is aimed at
* the pictures and the layout of the leaflet
* information about how to get to Oakwood.

Try to find examples of words used on the leaflet to back up your opinions.

The Grammar Class

Prepositions and Articles

Sentences are the key to success in writing and they need to be word perfect. **Prepositions** and **articles** are the nuts and bolts of well-built sentences – without these small bits and pieces the sentences may not hold together. They are not very interesting words on their own, but they are vital to the sense of a piece of writing.

Prepositions

A **preposition** is normally a single word that shows how one thing relates to another.

Look at the highlighted words in the sentences below.

Oakwood is clearly signposted off the A40 between Carmarthen and Haverfordwest.

Join the convoy at the Truck Depot.

100

The Writing Challenge

Designing a School Publicity Poster

Imagine that you could make your school sound as exciting and attractive as Oakwood Theme Park. Use your imagination to design and write a publicity poster for your school that makes it a must for everyone. Pick out parts of your school in detail and try to give them a new image.

The challenge

* design a poster
* make your school seem as interesting as a theme park
* use the words and phrases of advertising
* use clear and organized English
* make the most of the space available to include as much information as possible.

Writing Support

Here are ten tips to help you design and write your poster.

1	The writing frame has a horizontal band across the middle. Think of a dramatic banner headline for your school.
2	The page has been divided into eight triangular sections in a design that should catch the eye! You therefore need eight 'attractions' to advertise your school, no more, no less!
3	You might decide at a later point to change the design, making it different from the writing frame. That's OK, but use the writing frame as it stands to get you started.
4	Space is tight, but you still need to get a lot of information on your poster. This is your chance to ditch long sentences and come up instead with lots of strong phrases with no wasted words.

5 Don't just say – 'Canteen open at...' – but tell the reader some of what is on the menu.

6 You can play it straight – 'Vegetarians catered for' – or you can think of a send-up – 'Only the best sawdust in the burgers!'.

7 Cast your eye around the school. Think of a typical day for ideas – 'Once a day only – assembly! Don't miss it!'.

8 Use colour and small illustrations to make the poster attractive, but the information from the words and phrases is all-important.

9 You might be able to have a larger (A3) size page to work with. You may also be able to work on a computer. However, it is perfectly possible to do a brilliant poster by hand on A4 size paper.

10 Do not be abusive to the school and its teachers. After all, don't forget that you are one of the animals in the zoo!

Writing Frame

Your teacher will give you a writing frame like this one to help you plan your work.

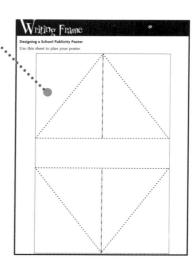

Unit 10
Healthy Eating for Children

Text

Healthy Eating For *Children*

FOOD ADVICE SERVICE
at TESCO

There's More!

262

STARTING YOUNG

Eating healthily is important for children. They need large amounts of calories and nutrients to meet their energy needs, for repair and maintenance and to fuel growth. Developing good eating habits in children early on will mean they are more likely to eat healthily as they grow up and reduce the risk of developing coronary heart disease and other illnesses in later life.

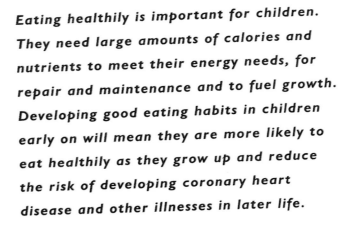

Healthy eating for young children is not the same as for adults. Children have smaller stomachs than adults, so they need smaller more regular meals. They also need more concentrated forms of calories and nutrients to make up a well-balanced diet.

This doesn't mean they can't have low-fat or reduced-fat products or fibre-providing foods. But they should not have too much of either of these.

FATS

While children shouldn't have a very low-fat diet, the balance of fats should be the same as for adults, cutting down on saturated fats in favour of unsaturated ones.

It is recommended that children under two years old have full-fat milk, but after that they can have semi-skimmed if the calories and nutrients are supplied by other sources in a healthy, varied diet. Skimmed milk can be introduced from the age of five.

SUGARS & TEETH

Children's teeth are most at risk from tooth decay, so try and avoid too many sweets, especially the sticky, chewy ones. Keep sweets and chocolates for meal times only - banning them altogether does not usually work. Dilute fruit juices or give them milk or fizzy water to drink. Make sure they brush their teeth after eating sweets and have a good dental care routine. Your dentist can give you more details.

VITAMINS & MINERALS

A good variety of foods should ensure children get all the vitamins and minerals they need. Iron is important for young children. Meat and dark-green vegetables are rich sources of iron. It is also found in bread, eggs, nuts and lentils.
Calcium and Vitamin D are important for growing children. Milk, cheese and yogurt are good sources of calcium (even low-fat varieties). It is also found in white bread, the soft bones of fish, e.g. canned sardines, and pulses such as baked beans. Vitamin D is found in foods like liver, oily fish and eggs. It is also made in the body by the action of sunlight on the skin.

There's More!

tips

healthy Eating

1. Only buy the foods you want your children to eat. Then let them make their own choices from the careful selection you provide.

2. Encourage children to get involved in planning and preparing meals e.g. For example children who help make their packed lunches are more likely to eat them.

3. Set an example by eating the right foods and having regular meal times. Make all meal times an occasion and avoid distractions such as television.

4. Make foods attractive and fun.

5. If your child doesn't like vegetables, try to disguise them in other foods e.g. soups, stews, moussaka.

6. Always grill food, especially meat products like sausages and burgers, choose the low-fat ones. Trim any excess fat from meat before cooking.

7. Unsalted nuts and raisins make ideal snacks for school lunch boxes.

8. Purée fresh, canned or frozen fruit and stir into yogurt or fromage frais for an easy dessert.

9. Make your own fish cakes using canned fish (such as tuna) and mashed potato. Don't forget to add an extra vegetable such as sweetcorn.

10. Give your children fruit for snacks instead of sweets. Choose smaller fruits such as small bananas, tangerines or small bunches of grapes. Make up a mini fruit basket for them, so they can make the choice themselves.

For any advice on food and health write to:
Food Advice Service, Tesco Stores Ltd, PO Box 18,
Cheshunt, Herts EN8 9SL.

The Reading Question

Tesco wants people to eat healthily and to shop at its stores.

How does the leaflet 'Healthy Eating For Children' try to persuade us to do so?

Talk about

* ❋ what the leaflet says about healthy eating
* ❋ what the leaflet says about unhealthy eating
* ❋ the way the leaflet is written and who it is aimed at
* ❋ the use of pictures, headings and sections
* ❋ what the leaflet tells you about Tesco.

See if you can find words and phrases from the leaflet to back up your opinions.

The Grammar Class

Controlling Sentences

When you are writing, try to control your sentences. You can do this in three ways.

* ❋ Don't make your sentences too long.
* ❋ Remember to use full stops at the end of each sentence.
* ❋ Use commas for pauses inside sentences.

A short sentence can be very effective. It can make a point strongly. You can then follow it with a slightly longer sentence to explain a detail. Look at the example below and note how the comma helps the second sentence.

Eating healthily is important for children. They need large amounts of calories and nutrients to meet their energy needs, for repair and maintenance and to fuel growth.

Task 1

The punctuation has been left out of the following two extracts from the Tesco leaflet.

Copy out each extract and add full stops and commas. You may use the leaflet to help you, but please note that you need to add more commas than you will find on the leaflet. Don't forget a capital letter to show the start of each new sentence.

1 healthy eating for young children is not the same as for adults / children have smaller stomachs than adults / so they need smaller / more regular meals / (add 2 full stops and 2 commas)

2 give your children fruit for snacks / instead of sweets / choose smaller fruits / such as small bananas / tangerines or small bunches of grapes / make up a mini fruit basket for them / so they can make the choice themselves /   (add 3 full stops and 4 commas)

In the next task, you will be working on a long sentence from the leaflet. In fact, don't tell Tesco, but it is too long! Very long sentences will leave readers lost and confused.

Task 2

Re-write the following sentence as two or three shorter sentences. Add and take away words and punctuation as you wish, but don't change the meaning.

Developing good eating habits in children early on will mean they are more likely to eat healthily as they grow up and reduce the risk of developing coronary heart disease and other illnesses later in life.

Concentrating on Commas

Commas mark pauses inside sentences, but where exactly? From the Tesco leaflet we can work out two 'rules'.

❀ Groups of words beginning with 'if', 'when', 'so' etc. (**conjunctions**) are usually marked off with commas.
❀ A comma is placed between items in a list instead of 'and' or 'or'.

If you go to a superstore these days, you can buy food, clothes, electrical goods and a lot more.

Here is a more general piece of advice.

Read your own work to yourself and judge the best places for pauses inside sentences. In some cases, it is your choice whether or not to use a comma.

Task 3

Re-write each sentence and put in the commas. The information in brackets tells you how many commas are needed.

1 If your child doesn't like vegetables try to disguise them in other foods.
(1 comma needed)
2 Children's teeth are most at risk from tooth decay so try and avoid too many sweets especially the sticky chewy ones.
(3 commas needed)
3 Iron is important for young children. It is found in meat dark-green vegetables bread eggs nuts and lentils.
(4 commas needed)

Singular and Plural Nouns

As you know, a **noun** is a naming word. It can be a person, a place or a thing. Do you know the difference between **singular** and **plural** nouns?

Singular means 'one' (think single); plural means 'more than one'.

I bought one bottle of water and half a dozen bottles of pop.

The common way to make a plural noun is to add 's' to the singular noun like this:

one bottle becomes two bottles

Task 4

Make the nouns in the following sentences into the correct plural form.

1 Children should develop good eating habit early in life.
2 Adult eat more than children.
3 You should clean your teeth after eating sweet.
4 Unsalted nut and raisin make ideal snack.

Most nouns have a straightforward plural, but some do not.

Some add 'es': **illness becomes illnesses**

Some lose 'y' and add 'ies': **variety becomes varieties**

Some lose 'f' or 'fe' and add 'ves': **life becomes lives**

Beware! Many nouns do not fit any of the above 'rules'! Do your best with the following task.

Task 5

Write down the plural of the following nouns.

bunch ✎✎✎   knife ✎✎✎

lunch ✎✎✎   half ✎✎✎

punch ✎✎✎   loaf ✎✎✎

box ✎✎✎   tooth ✎✎✎

potato ✎✎✎   foot ✎✎✎

tomato ✎✎✎   child ✎✎✎

body ✎✎✎   man ✎✎✎

baby ✎✎✎   woman ✎✎✎

The Writing Challenge

Designing and Writing a Leaflet

Young people do not get enough exercise. They sit at home playing computer games and watching videos. Design and write a leaflet that persuades teenagers to take their fitness seriously. Write about the good habits and the bad habits of young people.

The challenge

* design a leaflet, using the Tesco leaflet as a model
* provide interesting material
* create a lively style and tone of voice for the leaflet
* use accurate English.

Writing Support

You might find the following statements about teenage fitness helpful as a starting point. You could include some of these quotations (or others you have researched yourself) in your leaflet.

'P.E and games at school is boring. You have to play in a team and half the people stand around and treat it as a joke. I want to keep fit, but I don't get the chance.' Dean, aged 15

'All of my friends smoke, so I smoke as well. I'd feel left out of the gang if I didn't. I only smoke a few a day anyway.' Shelley, aged 13

'Kids are spending more and more of their time in front of the video or playing computer games. Instead of real sport they settle for virtual sport.' **A doctor**

'You don't have to be a proper athlete to get exercise. Skateboarding, street hockey, five-a-side football, aerobics... just get out of the house and do something. Get down the sports centre and open your eyes!' Sam, aged 14

'Girls now can have their own teams in football, cricket and rugby. We don't have to stand on the touchline cheering for the boys. If you haven't caught up, get it sorted.' Jodie, aged 13

Writing Frame

Your teacher will give you writing frames like these to .... help you plan your work.

Unit 11
Hens and Eggs

But not all hens get the chance to live this way.

Nearly all the eggs you buy in the supermarket are laid by hens which are known as 'battery hens'. They live in tiny, cramped cages, called 'battery cages'. As many as five hens have to spend most of their lives in just one cage. And lots of these cages are stacked together in big farm buildings. Battery hens don't have such a good life...

● each hen has to live in a space as small as the cover of a telephone book

● they cannot move around or preen their feathers properly

● they cannot flap or stretch out their wings

● they have nowhere to dust-bathe

● they have to stand on a wire floor which can hurt their feet and damage their claws

● they may get pecked and bullied by others but cannot get away from them

It's like having to spend the rest of your life in a telephone box with two other people!

Because people like eating eggs and they want to be able to buy them cheaply. So farmers have to produce lots of eggs to sell at low prices in supermarkets.

And at the moment, keeping battery hens is the cheapest way for them to do this.

That's horrible. So why are hens kept like this?

Are there other ways of keeping the hens that lay eggs?

What are the differences between perchery or barn hens and free-range hens?

Yes. Some hens are kept in large barns and not in cages. They're called perchery or barn hens, or free-range hens.

Perchery or barn hens have:		Free-range hens have:
✓	a perch to roost on	✓
sometimes	litter, dirt and earth where they can scratch, peck and dust-bathe	✓
✓	room to flap their wings, stretch and preen their feathers	✓
✓	a nest box to lay eggs in peace and quiet	✓
✗	the freedom to go outside in the fresh air during the day	✓

But hens that are kept this way need more space and more looking after, which is expensive for farmers, so the eggs cost a little more in the shops.

Egg quiz

Here are some boxes of eggs like the ones you might find on a supermarket shelf. Can you tell which ones were laid by hens kept in battery cages?

Country FRESH EGGS — A

Free-Range Eggs — B

C — FRESHLY LAID EGGS

FRESH PERCHERY EGGS — D

E — barn eggs

Fresh FARM eggs — F

(Answer: A, C and F all come from battery hens. If the box does not actually say that the eggs are barn, perchery or free-range, they have probably been laid by battery hens.)

The RSPCA believes that hens should not suffer through having to live in battery cages.

In June 1999 European Union Agriculture Ministers agreed to ban the conventional battery cage by 1 January 2012. After this time only enriched cages and alternative systems will be allowed.

The RSPCA wants:

✓ **A development programme for the introduction of properly designed alternatives.**

✓ **All egg boxes to be labelled to show clearly which eggs come from battery hens.**

✓ **To help farmers change to ways of keeping hens which are better for the hens, by asking people to buy barn, perchery or free-range eggs.**

Animal action

What you can do

- NEVER buy battery eggs.

- Show this fact-sheet to your friends and family. Ask them to stop buying battery eggs.

- Write to your local Member of the European Parliament (MEP). You can get his/her name and address from your local library.

- Look out for the Freedom Food mark on free-range and barn (perchery) egg boxes. Freedom Food is a farm animal welfare labelling scheme developed by the RSPCA. It ensures farm animals are properly cared for throughout their lives.

Here are some tips on how to write your letter:

- Write how you feel about battery cages and why you think they are cruel. You can use the information in this fact-sheet but try to write about it in your own words and remember to sign your name at the bottom

- Ask your MEP how he or she feels about hens kept in battery cages. Ask him or her to write back to you and tell you what he or she is doing to help. Don't forget your name and address!

- Don't write too much. Keep your letter as short and clear as possible.

PLEASE HELP US TO STOP HENS SUFFERING THROUGH BEING KEPT IN BATTERY CAGES.

Join the RSPCA's Animal Action Club. We'll send you your own Animal Action Pack and regular copies of Animal Action magazine, so you can help us to help all animals. Write to the club at the address below.

Causeway
Horsham
West Sussex
RH12 1HG
Telephone
01403 264181
Registered charity
no. 219099
*We receive no State
or lottery aid*
P39 8.97
Website: http://www.rspca.org.uk (From October 1997)   Illustrated by Jane Gedye

The Reading Question

How does the RSPCA try to teach us about hens and eggs?

Talk about

❋ the information on the fact-sheet about battery hens and other hens
❋ the way the fact-sheet is designed
❋ the way the fact-sheet tries to persuade us to take action.

See if you can find examples from the fact-sheet to back up your opinions.

The Grammar Class

Homophones

A **homophone** is a word that sounds the same as another word, but which is spelt differently. The words 'to', 'too' and 'two' all sound the same, but in writing they are different. If you make the wrong choice from the homophones 'to', 'too' and 'two', you are making an error of grammar rather than a spelling mistake.

Look at the homophones in the following sentence.

They have to stand on a wire floor which can hurt their feet and damage their claws.

All of the highlighted words are correctly spelt here, but a sentence like this could easily contain lots of homophone errors.

Do you sometimes mix up 'their', 'there' and 'they're'? What about 'your' and 'you're'? Or 'it's' and 'its'?

Do you spell 'which' correctly or do you confuse it with 'witch' (broomsticks and halloween!)?

Task 1

Choose one of the homophones from the brackets to fill each gap. Then copy out the completed sentences.

1 Are 〰〰〰 other ways of keeping the hens that lay eggs?
〰〰〰 called perchery or barn hens, or free-range hens.
They stretch out and flap 〰〰〰 wings.
(there/their/they're)
2 Write 〰〰〰 your local Member of Parliament.
Don't write 〰〰〰 much!
It's like having 〰〰〰 spend the rest of your life in a telephone box with 〰〰〰 other people! (to/two/too)
3 Each hen 〰〰〰 to live in a space 〰〰〰 small 〰〰〰 the cover of a telephone book. (as/has)

Task 2

Correct the homophone errors in the sentences below. The number of errors in each sentence is shown in brackets.

1 The RSPCA believes that hens should not suffer threw having two live in battery cages. (2)
2 Never by battery eggs. (1)
3 They make a nest so they have a quite place too lay there eggs. (3)
4 They stretch out and flap there wings. (1)
5 We'll send you you're own Animal Action Pack. (1)

There are many small groups of homophones. Some are less obvious than others, because the words are not always pronounced exactly the same.

Here are some examples:

where	were	we're
of	off	've (have)
as	has	
is	his	

The list goes on.

Some people might argue that these are not 'real' homophones, but there is no doubt that lots of errors occur when they are used.

You can use grammar to explain why a homophone may be a wrong choice. Some explanations are harder than others! The easiest ones to explain and check are the ones with **apostrophes**.

'We're' is really 'we are' and so it should not be confused with 'where' and 'were'. 'Could've' and 'should've' are shortened forms of 'could have' and 'should have'.

Don't write 'could of'!

Task 3

Make up your own sentences to show that you can use the following homophones correctly.

1	where/were/we're	6	write/right
2	of/off/'ve	7	it's/its
3	no/know/now	8	lose/loose
4	knew/new	9	our/are
5	here/hear	10	see/sea

The Writing Challenge

Writing a Discursive Essay

How should animals be treated by humans?

Think about your answer to this question and write a discursive essay (in other words, discuss in writing).

Discursive essays are not easy to write - you answer the question by giving your opinions, but you need plenty of ideas and examples to back these up. You must say what you believe, but you must also try to persuade anyone who reads your essay to agree with you. To do this, you must argue thoughtfully and with understanding. It is important to try to imagine someone reading your essay who might not have the same views as you.

Write about one or more animal welfare or animal cruelty topics in your essay.

Everyone has opinions about animals - many people regard them as almost the equals of human beings, but some people behave badly towards them. There are many animal welfare issues to consider: scientific experiments on animals; unwanted pets; the transportation of calves; and so on.

The challenge

* organize your essay properly into paragraphs
* give your opinions and explain yourself clearly
* back up your opinions with examples
* show you can express yourself in clear, well-constructed sentences
* show you have strong feelings, but are sensible too
* persuade the reader to agree with you.

Writing Support

Here is a piece written by a pupil on the subject of greyhound racing.

Read it through and also read the teacher's comment at the end.
How could this piece of writing be improved?
What else would you include?

Now write your own discursive essay on an 'animal' subject that you feel strongly about.

Animal Rights – The Treatment of Greyhounds

Some people who breed and race greyhounds mistreat the animals. These people don't care about if they don't get enough food or if they don't get enough medical treatment when they need it. They train these animals and when they are training them they abuse them if they don't do as the trainers want. When the greyhounds don't win a race after about three races, they abuse them, then dump them somewhere and leave them to die with no food or water.

I feel strongly about this topic because I have got a whippet that we found up the mountain and she was only three months old. She was really thin and she was covered in tarmac which had set on her fur and her ears were burnt. We took her home and then up to the vets to get her treated and the vet said that we could keep her.

I get really upset when I see animals on TV that have been abused and I can't understand why someone would do that to a poor innocent animal for no reason.

Excellent topic, strong personal feelings well-expressed. Some of your sentences ramble a little and you use words like 'they' a bit loosely. It would be easy to put these things right. Very good effort so far!